The Birds of Colonsay and Oronsay

D.C. Jardine

Contents

Introduction	3
Where & How to see Colonsay's Birds	5
Suggested 'Hotspots'	10
Herons	16
Geese	18
"Colonsay's Duck"	20
Birds of Prey	22
Farming & Birds	28
Seabirds	36
Checklist & Status	41
Further Reading	48

Copyright © D.C. Jardine 2002
ISBN 1 899863 32 X
Printed in Great Britain

Introduction

It is over 15 years since *The Birds of Colonsay and Oransay* was published and available copies are now becoming scarce. This new guide seeks to provide fresh information for visitors and is based on the results of studies on Colonsay's birds during the period since the last booklet was produced.

On the island it has been a period of change in farming and other land management and in the financial structures that support them. This has led to some interesting changes in the composition of the bird-life on the islands.

Perhaps the largest and most encouraging change has been the reversal of the fortunes of two of the crows. In the mid 1980s the Chough was a very scarce breeder and Hooded Crows were common-place; now the Chough, while not abundant, is more common than the Hoodie. Few visitors can fail to notice the geese on the islands; Greylag, formerly only winter visitors, are now breeding. The seabird colonies have increased in size and summer visitors interested in birds will remember well the sights (and smell!) of the colonies on the west coast.

Many people have commented that one of the most useful features of *The Birds of Colonsay and Oransay* was its section on birdwatching by car or bicycle. This was because many visitors want to know where they may see some of the special birds on the island; indeed for some they provide a highlight of their holidays. Any advice that helps the visitor to see these specialities has to be tempered with the understanding that the information provided will not cause the birds themselves any harm. It is to be hoped that the expanded guidance provided in the section "Where and How to See Colonsay's Birds" will protect the needs of the birds and yet provide useful tips to those who want to see more.

Another of the merits of *The Birds of Colonsay and Oransay* was its comprehensive species list, which allowed visitors to check their sightings against the status of the species on the islands. This new book is different and is not meant to act as a field-guide to the birds of the island but does include a brief checklist of the recent status of the birds on the islands; this can be used to assist in the verification of sightings.

I hope that you find this new volume useful and that it will help you enjoy your visit and to look after the interests of the birds of these special islands.

David Jardine

Acknowledgements

Many different people have assisted in the preparation of *Colonsay's Birds*. The tolerant attitude of landowners, farmers and crofters on the islands has allowed the author to study the birds with few restrictions; this is greatly appreciated. Family members have both introduced the author to the island and given invaluable support during many visits; this has brought many happy memories. The ringing studies have been facilitated by the British Trust for Ornithology who run the ringing scheme. Images were kindly provided by Margaret Staley, Tristan Farquhar and the RSPB. Cover picture by Julia Page.

Where and How to See Colonsay's Birds

Most of Colonsay's birds can be seen without ever leaving the road or one of the suggested walks for the island. The booklet *Exploring Colonsay* (No 11 in the West Highland Series) gives details of various walks, which let you discover Colonsay's special qualities. They are also good routes to see many of the birds. Some of the special nooks and crannies on these walks and where it is worth having a look for more interesting birds are given later. We shall start with a trip round Colonsay's road network.

At the harbour in Scalasaig, except in summer, there is always a chance of seeing a Great Northern Diver or Black Guillemot close in to the shore and, during summer, the Common Sandpiper will be heard as it dashes excitedly around its territory.

Take the road up past the shop and for the next mile or so, where the scrubby hillside comes down to the gardens of the houses, most of the common garden birds can be seen – thrushes, tits, Robin and Dunnock and towards Glassard you may hear a Whitethroat sing in the scrub during spring and early summer.

Up the hill to Loch Turraman the bleak heather hillside gives cover to a few Pheasants and an occasional Sparrowhawk may be seen gliding through on its way down to the scrub area. Loch Turraman is a good place to see Tufted Duck, although they are now less common than a few years ago; on one occasion an Osprey was also seen there.

Just down from the loch, stop at the 'Z' bend and look down over East Loch Fada and across to Colonsay House woodlands. From this vantage point there are regular sightings of Heron, Mallard, Teal, Goldeneye, Greylag Goose, Whooper Swan, Buzzard and Golden Eagle.

Birds in Colonsay's History

The earliest of these is from the 14th century when King David II made a grant that refers to (Peregrine) "falcon eyries in the islands of Colonsay". Another early record was pointed out by Seton Gordon in *Afoot in the Hebrides*. He writes of a Raven on the mainmast of a ship on one of the gravestones at Oronsay Priory; all of the stones with boats are clear and have no birds but perhaps he means the C16th stone shown here, which is difficult to interpret. Another well known bird is the gull (legend does not identify the species) which betrayed the location of Malcolm MacPhee's hiding place on Seal Island on Oronsay to the invading Coll Ciotach MacDonald and led to his capture and murder in 1623.

After you cross the causeway between East Loch Fada and Mid Loch Fada, pull in. Occasional sightings of Red-throated Diver and Cormorant are recorded in this area. In the reed beds during the summer you should see or hear Reed Buntings and Sedge Warbler, and in the nearby fields Skylark, Lapwing and Snipe. As you approach Kiloran Farm there are usually good views to be had of finches such as Greenfinch, Chaffinch and Linnet.

Follow the road to the junction and turn right, then bear left past Kiloran Farm and the gates of Colonsay House. In the fields before Kiloran Bay, Greylag and Canada Geese and sometimes Barnacle and White-fronted Geese, and Curlew can be seen in good numbers from October to early May.

At the far end of the fields the road turns left and climbs towards Uragaig. Stop at the parking area overlooking Kiloran Bay with its great sweep of golden sand, Atlantic rollers and huge sand-dunes. Thousands of Kittiwakes come in to bathe where the burn runs into the bay during the summer, Choughs feed on the dunes, and beyond the breakers look for Fulmar and other seabirds. Occasionally in winter other birds such as Common Scoter and Long-tailed Duck can be seen here.

Retrace your route to the junction just past Kiloran Farm and instead of turning left, go straight on towards Kilchattan. This will take you past the remains of a plantation, which was blown down during a winter gale, to the old mill. From the point where you entered the woods at Colonsay House to here, is where you are most likely to see Spotted Flycatcher, Treecreeper, Coal Tit and Goldcrest.

Passing through Upper Kilchattan, check West Loch Fada. The fields often have geese, even in summer and, in winter, this loch is where you are most likely to find Pochard. You can get excellent views from the road, which is about 20m above the loch.

Why are there no Puffins on Colonsay?

With so many seabirds breeding on Colonsay it is perhaps surprising that there are no Puffins. Their absence is thought to be due to ground predators such as rats and cats, which inhabit their burrows and prevent their breeding. For this reason Puffins are restricted to only a few places in Argyll such as the Treshnish Isles and Sanda. Puffins can be seen on Colonsay: it is sometimes possible to find single birds on the sea at Pigs Paradise, but this can be like looking for the proverbial needle in a haystack amongst the Guillemots and Razorbills. Other times to look for them are during ferry crossings or on seawatches from headlands on the west coast when they can sometimes be seen in late summer.

At Port Mór, just below the cemetery, the road runs within a few feet of the weed-covered boulder beach. There is room to park for a few minutes and quietly watch for Shelduck, Eider, Shag, Redshank and Turnstone.

The next view-point overlooks the Golf Course and Machrins Bay. This area usually has Raven, Wheatear, Oystercatcher and other waders. Outside the breeding season, it is a good site for Golden Plover.

Having passed Machrins Farm, the stretch from the 'S' bend to the next road junction is a good area for Whitethroat, Whinchat and Willow Warbler. A variety of birds can be seen along the road, which branches off to the right to 'The Strand', including Cuckoo, Meadow Pipit and Stonechat.

The Strand is one of the best places for seeing waders and, depending on the season, many species mentioned earlier can be seen as well as Ringed Plover, Dunlin, Greenshank and Bar-tailed Godwit. If you park there as the tide is coming in, it is quite easy to watch at least 15 species from the car; many birds will come within a few yards of a vehicle. On such quiet occasions, as many as four species of birds of prey have been seen including Peregrine, Merlin and Hen Harrier.

In the course of a leisurely ride around the island and without ever walking more than a few steps from the road, it is possible for the average birdwatcher to see at least 50 species in a day. A more experienced observer, when seeking out the special spots could well be rewarded with 70 species.

During recent years the number of visitors to the island has increased, particularly in the breeding season. Free access has allowed people to enjoy all aspects of the islands, including birdlife. Some species, however, are being disturbed to the limit of their tolerance and may disappear altogether: it is almost 10 years since Golden Eagles last successfully reared young on Colonsay. Please help protect the birds – PLEASE KEEP YOUR DISTANCE.

Wildlife Crime

Crime is unusual on Colonsay, but one of the few court cases relating to the island was for wildlife crime. It involved the theft of a clutch of eggs from one of the rarest birds breeding on the islands – Chough. In April 2002, at Thames Court in London, a Mr Gonshaw was convicted of stealing this clutch and sentenced to 3 months imprisonment. Please consider carefully whom you tell about the rare birds that you see, particularly if you find a nest site. Others have been known to abuse such information and the birds suffer. "Careless talk costs lives!"

Some of the most interesting species on Colonsay can take a little more effort to locate. One of the best ways to find a number of these birds is to go out on a still spring or summer evening, particularly at dusk and listen – it is best to stick to the road in the fading light. Some birds, such as Grasshopper Warblers, are likely only to be heard, but you should be rewarded by the sight of a Woodcock around Colonsay House, and if you are lucky, a Long-eared Owl hunting. In June it is sometimes possible to hear the calls of their young in the woodlands as they beg for food.

If you are particularly interested in passage seabirds the best spots in autumn have proved to be Ardskenish Point, Dubh Eilean at the north end, and Eilean Treadhrach on Oronsay – all of these are a bit inaccessible. Garbh Claddich and Rubh Aird Alanais can be reached more easily in the early morning when passage is most active. A north west wind following a strong south westerly often gives the most interesting watching.

Suggested 'hotspots' on the walks in the West Highland Series – *Exploring Colonsay.*

Kiloran Bay and Carnan Eoin – Walk 1
Despite its scenic beauty, the beach at Kiloran Bay is not one of the best birdwatching spots on the island as the sand, along with the constant pounding by the waves, is somewhat sterile giving little feeding. The freshwater burn is a common washing place for Kittiwakes in summer and there are often a few Eiders offshore. The dunes and the hill below Carnan Eoin are often more interesting as the dung from out-wintered cattle gives rich feeding. It is one of the best places on the islands for seeing the flock of young (non-breeding) Chough.

Uragaig and Loch an Sgoltaire – Walk 2
The walk out to the Uragaig cliffs takes one to the most accessible area for seeing many of the islands' seabirds. This area has the main colony of Fulmars, which prefer the ledges on the upper parts of the grassy cliffs. Guillemots, Razorbills, Kittiwakes and Shags all nest lower down on the rocky cliffs. Black Guillemots are less common and are often best seen by looking for them on the sea, close inshore, as they remain hidden when nesting in holes and caves.

Lost at Sea

On 1 January 1897 a bird that had never been seen alive in Britain before was found by a roadside stream between Kiloran and Kilchattan. It was a female White-faced Petrel, or Frigate Petrel, which normally lives in the southern oceans and as far north as the Canaries. It had been blown to Colonsay by severe south-westerly gales which preceded its arrival on the island. Only one other has ever been seen in Britain, offshore from Cornwall in August 1963.

Beyond Uragaig croft it is worthwhile keeping your eyes (and ears) open for the distinctive Hebridean finch, the Twite, whose nasal call is often the first clue of its presence – the bright pink rump of the males makes them more than just a little brown bird. On the return by Loch Sgoltaire Canada Geese can often be seen and this hill loch also has Tufted Duck. Birds tend to feed in the shallower area near the water treatment plant.

Balnahard & Dunan na Nighean – Walk 3

The Balnahard walk is long, but rewarding, with much of interest throughout. The climb up past Carnan Eoin is a good place to look out for Jackdaws which nest on its steep craggy southern slope. Down towards Balnahard, where the track goes close to Port Sgibinis, is one of the few spots in the north of the island where Shelduck are regularly seen. This seaweedy beach is worth looking at closely as it occasionally has small birds on the shore; it is a good place for finding White Wagtails in spring and autumn as they migrate to and from Iceland.

Round toward Balnahard Farm try listening for Corncrake in summer. Keep one eye on the skies in this area as Buzzard, Kestrel, Peregrine and Sparrowhawk all regularly hunt here. There is often a Great Northern Diver swimming in Balnahard Bay and Ringed Plovers are regularly on the shore.

Balnahard – Walk 4

The dunes at Balnahard are always a good place to see Chough. Wheatears and Ringed Plovers nest here. The higher ground to the north is an interesting area where Lapwings are still breeding and Golden Plover are often found here outside the breeding season.

If you do venture right to the north end of the island it is always worth searching the sea just to the north of Colonsay as the mixing of the sea currents here means that there are usually congregations of seabirds and once, in autumn, 9 Grey Phalaropes were seen.

Colonsay House Circuit – Walk 5
This is always an interesting walk particularly down the east side of Loch Fada and into Colonsay House policies. In poor weather it can often be the best place for shelter, but to find most of the woodland birds, early on a fine spring morning will be most rewarding.

Take your time at East Loch Fada as birds hide in the reed-bed, and be patient – Dabchicks will often appear, and the squeals of Water Rail can be heard.

The birches and alders at the east end of the loch are a favourite spot for Lesser Redpolls and recently Long-tailed Tits have become established here. Further into the woods it is worth listening for Chiffchaffs and Blackcaps, which are easier to find by using their song, than by sight in the dense tree and rhododendron cover.

The walk by Riasg Buidhe can be relatively quiet for birds but there are often Snipe in the marshy ground and Buzzards or Raven overhead.

The Strand & Dun Cholla – Walk 6
This is a wonderful circular walk which takes you to a number of interesting bird areas and there is a good chance of seeing otters here as the sea is often calm, being well sheltered from the west.

The sea to the south east of Beinn Eibhe is always worth checking carefully – some of the best congregations of Eider are usually found feeding in these shallow waters. They are usually accompanied by Red-breasted Mergansers and divers (three species have been seen here in spring). Sometimes there are more unusual species such as Common Scoter and Slavonian Grebes to be found in the Eider flocks.

Loch Cholla is another place worth scanning, although birds are often well hidden in the aquatic vegetation. Teal rest on the loch and the reedbed is usually the home to a few Sedge Warblers and Reed Buntings.

The Yanks are coming

There are a number of North American birds that have turned up on Colonsay. The first of these was a Yellow-billed Cuckoo found in November 1904. More recently a Killdeer was found at Kiloran meadow in January 1984, an American Golden Plover at Traigh nam Barc in October 1993. All these records show that rare vagrants from the other side of the Atlantic do occur on Colonsay. With the large area of sheltered woodland on the island it is likely only to be a matter of time until one of the North American passerines is found in the autumn. Happy hunting!

The Western Cliffs – Walk 7

These cliffs are the best place to see (and smell) seabirds in their thousands. The large concentration often attracts a few Arctic Skuas in summer and you should scan high in the sky for them soaring over the cliffs before they plunge to rob food from the returning Kittiwakes and Guillemots. Arctic Skuas do not breed on Colonsay; these birds are from remote moors on Jura and occasionally can been seen crossing over Colonsay making their way to the western cliffs to carry out their piracy.

Machrins and Ardskenish – Walk 8

The walk over the Golf Course is pleasant and a good place to keep an eye open for birds – Chough feed here and Golden Plover and Curlew are regular in winter.

Ardskenish, with its big skies, always gives a sense of isolation. For this reason it is an exciting place to visit. The skerries offshore to the west often have nesting terns which feed close inshore and, near the point, it is possible to watch Gannets and Manx Shearwater pass in large numbers in the spring and autumn; in autumn they are sometimes joined by Storm Petrels or Sooty Shearwaters. A telescope will help identification, as in certain conditions they can be well offshore.

Small bays on the east side of the Ardskenish peninsula, and Traigh nam Barc, are amongst the best sites for seeing waders on the island. Dunlin and Turnstone are regularly seen here, and Sanderling and Golden Plovers are not uncommon. Look out here especially for the many unusual waders such as Little Stint and Curlew Sandpiper; American Golden Plover have even been seen here.

Birdwatching from the Ferry

The passage to and from Colonsay can provide an excellent opportunity to see some of the seabirds which are scarcer visitors to the island. While it is not possible to give definitive advice, there are certain circumstances which are helpful. Evening crossings to, or from, Oban in summer are amongst the best for seeing Manx Shearwaters as they gather in rafts to the west of the Garvellochs, sometimes in large numbers, and their wheeling flights can easily be seen as they are disturbed by the ferry. Small numbers can also be seen in flight closer to Colonsay. Other oceanic species such as Storm Petrels are less regular and are usually associated with poor weather conditions; in autumn they are sometimes joined by Sooty Shearwaters. Skuas, either Arctic or Great, are likely to be seen at any point on the crossing south of Easdail; the former are more common. Often the best opportunity for seeing Puffins is from the Ferry, with the stretch of sea to the south of the Garvellochs being the most likely spot. On most crossings during the summer months given favourable conditions it is likely that you will see cetaceans – Harbour Porpoise, Minke Whale and Bottlenose Dolphins are all possibilities.

Oronsay
The Royal Society for the Protection of Birds now lease the farm on Oronsay where they farm to help the birds there. It is a good place to hear Corncrake and see Chough. They have produced a useful leaflet guide to the island, which provides helpful information. Copies can usually be obtained from the Shop or the Hotel on Colonsay.

Herons

There are only a few Grey Herons on Colonsay and Oronsay, with the total population never exceeding 15 pairs that are usually spread between 2 or 3 different Heronries. On the mainland Herons nest in tall trees, but this is not their usual nesting habitat on the islands. It is not that there are no suitable trees on Colonsay for Herons have nested in the small wood to the west of Scalasaig in the past and may indeed do so again in the future. Rather, they currently nest in small bushes, reedbeds and on a ruined building on Seal Island, off Oronsay. The Heronries are transitory with at least seven different sites being used over the last 25 years, each being used for a number of years as the population increases from one or two pairs before declining into disuse. The reason for this pattern is not known but may reflect the life history of individual adult birds.

Nordic Winter

Little is know of the movements of Herons on Colonsay and the other islands of the west coast of Scotland. So it came as a great surprise when one of the chicks ringed on Colonsay in spring 2000 was found in southern Norway in February 2001 after a period of heavy snowfall. This is only the third ever British ringed Heron to be found in Norway; the other two, less surprisingly, being ringed in the Shetlands.

In early spring the flimsy twig nests are built and the pale blue eggs are laid. On Colonsay the normal clutch size is 3–4 eggs (range 2–6). It is unusual for all of these eggs to produce young; poor weather during the nestling stages can lead to losses and it is the norm for only 1–2 young to be reared from each nest.

Most of the heronries are in inaccessible locations but as this species can be prone to disturbance it is best to keep a safe distance from the nests.

Geese

In 1934, Malcolm Clark, the gamekeeper, trying to improve the number of wildfowl wintering on the islands, introduced two pairs of Canada Geese to Colonsay. Their loud calls were thought to persuade migrating geese to land and remain. They bred successfully and numbers had risen to 65 by the late 1960s and for a number of years Colonsay was one of only about four sites in Scotland where they were found. While the population on Colonsay has remained fairly static since then, the population in the rest of Scotland has increased steadily and it is now widespread. On Colonsay a peak of around 100 birds was reached but in recent years has dropped back to around 60. Pairs nest in coastal moorland and take their young to nearby lochs or the sea shortly after hatching. The main concentrations are around Loch Sgoltaire, near Baleromin Dhu and on the islets around the Strand and Oronsay.

The Greylag Goose, while often being seen in the pastures around the islands is less confiding when breeding. Breeding was first recorded in 1986 when three pairs were found. They prefer the offshore islets around the Strand, Ardskenish and Oronsay with over 30 goslings being found in some years. With this growth in breeding birds its status has changed in the last twenty years from wintering in modest (c30) numbers to a resident population of around 200 birds which has only been kept in check by the occasional bird being shot in winter.

While Greylag and Canada are often the more visible geese on the islands, they are not the most common; Barnacle and White-fronted winter in much larger numbers. These species arrive back in mid-October from their breeding grounds in Greenland and the passage of large numbers of birds en route for Islay is a memorable spectacle of autumn.

Around 400 Barnacle Geese usually winter, although over 650 have been recorded. The presence of ringed birds show that there is regular interchange between birds on Colonsay and Oronsay and the large numbers wintering on Islay. The Barnacle are the most timid of the geese, usually feeding on Oronsay or at Ardskenish. The White-fronted Geese usually return around the same time as the Barnacle and they winter in pastures around the island. There are rarely more than 250 present. The wintering geese usually depart during mid-April.

"Colonsay's Duck"

The Eider has long been known as the "Colonsay Duck", with the *Lach Colonsa* quoted by Gray in the 19th century. This represents its very favourable status on Colonsay at that time, but the true origin of its name is not clear. Another name, *Lach Lochlannach* appears to be much older, meaning "Men of the Loch" Duck (Men of the Loch/Lough being both Scots & Irish Gaelic for Vikings, Norse or Scandinavian people.) This name is probably the source of the suggestion that Eider were brought in from Norway at the end of the 9th century by Vikings or at least were associated with them in some way. It is difficult to be sure of the true origin of Eider on Colonsay, but it is interesting to note that no trace of Eider has been reported amongst the bird remains found in the excavations of the mesolithic shell middens on Oronsay. As the first records in the literature are in 1549, by Dean Munro, the possibility of the Eider being amongst the earliest bird introductions cannot be ruled out.

Whatever their origin, the name "Colonsay Duck" is appropriate as the expansion and population growth of Eiders

spreading out from Colonsay and Oronsay, from about 1870, led to the colonisation of Kintyre and the Firth of Clyde. On these, and adjacent Inner Hebrides, many of the breeding populations were regularly harvested for their eggs, with records of eggs from Islay, and to a lesser extent from Tiree and Coll, being sent to market in Glasgow. In contrast, the breeding colonies on Colonsay and Oronsay were given special protection, by Lord Colonsay.

Nowadays 100–150 pairs of Eider breed each year. Most are found around the islets and sheltered bays of Oronsay and southern Colonsay. Most of the population gather to feed in the shallow water to the east of the Strand in the early spring. On still days the sound of their display is a wonderful harbinger of spring. These sheltered areas are ideal places for the Eider to gather their family crèches. Yearly counts around Ardskenish in June show that usually between a third and two thirds of the females have young and while there is some variation in the annual mean brood size there is little variation in the number of young per female.

Birds of prey

Seven birds of prey occur regularly on Colonsay and Oronsay, another two species the White-tailed Eagle and Osprey, occur occasionally, while a further five have been recorded on just a single occasion. Following reintroduction of the White-tailed Eagle and an increase in its population in Scotland, it is possible that in a few years the "Erne" will regularly be seen on the islands. It is always worth keeping an eye open for this flying "barn-door" with its white tail, but be careful not to confuse it with a young Golden Eagle, which may be paying a visit from neighbouring Jura or Mull.

Common Buzzard
This species lives up to its name as it is by far the most common bird of prey on the islands. This has not always been the case with few occurring early in the 20th century. By the 1930s, three or four pairs had become established on Colonsay and by the

> ### Buzzards replace Kestrels
>
> In the late 19th and early 20th century the Kestrel was the commonest bird of prey on the islands. It is now far from common, with usually only one pair attempting to breed some summers. One explanation for this change is the increase in Buzzards that compete with Kestrels for nesting sites on crags. In addition, a reduction in grain crops and increased levels of grazing have both served to reduce their main food supply - small mammals such as Wood Mice and House Mice. Kestrels are still seen migrating through the islands particularly in the early spring and during September – Balnahard and around the Strand are usually good places to see them.

early 1960s the population had risen to five or six pairs. Since then there has been a significant increase in the population to around 20 pairs from the 1980s.

From the mid-1980s the breeding performance of Buzzards on Colonsay and Oronsay has been studied by trying to locate every breeding pair on the islands. Young have been measured to establish the egg hatching date. Some of the young have also been ringed. The number of pairs present each year varied between 17 and 24 pairs; the number of successful pairs varied between 6 and 20, leading to significant annual variation in the number of young reared. The average number of young reared varied between 1.4 – 2.5 young per successful nesting attempt. There was little variation in the average annual hatching date, which was between 22 –31 May.

Around 7% of the birds ringed have been re-found: all have been on Colonsay and Oronsay except two, which were found on Mull (29km away) and in Ayrshire (92km).

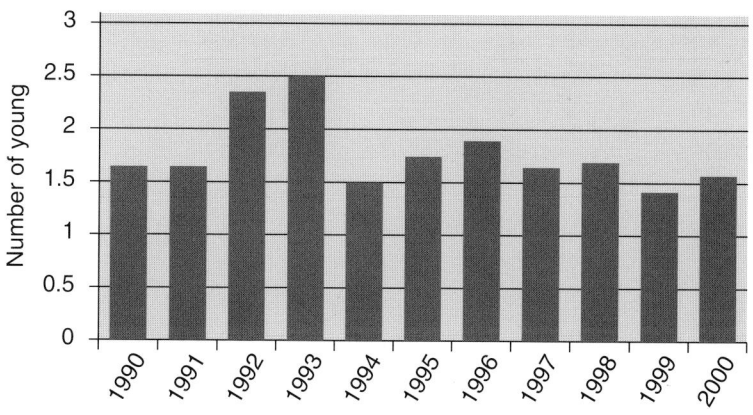

Variation in average Buzzard brood size from successful nests

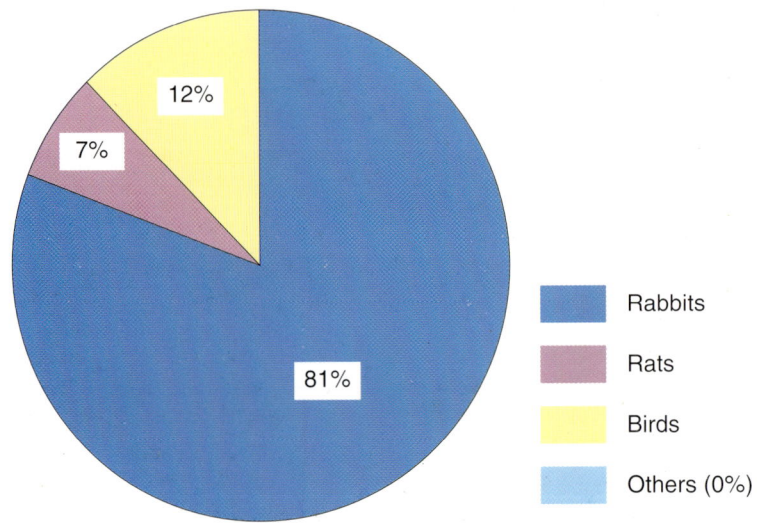

Buzzard prey – Colonsay 1989–2000

The study also investigated what Buzzards feed on. Rabbit prey comprised the main food item found at nests and from 1990 –2000 a measure of the rabbit population was established by sampling in the main machair areas. This study showed that there was a relationship between the proportion of rabbit in prey remains and the level of the rabbit population. In years when there were fewer rabbits there was a higher proportion of birds and rats in the diet of the young.

The study sought to establish whether the variation in annual breeding performance was a consequence of changes in the availability of food, but no relationships were found between Buzzard breeding parameters (hatch date, average brood) and the level of rabbit population. Another explanation of the variation in breeding could be the weather during the breeding season; but analysis of the weather records from Colonsay did not indicate any relationship between Buzzard breeding and various climatic parameters (spring rainfall, early summer sunshine). It appears that the causes of annual variation in Buzzard breeding are complex and may involve both food supplies and weather. More information (and complex analyses!) will be required before these can be untangled.

Merlin and Hen Harrier
The Merlin and Hen Harrier have not been found nesting on Colonsay and Oronsay in recent years – they are more common in winter. The Merlins are probably birds from the Icelandic breeding population, which are known to winter in Scotland. The harriers are more local; they are likely to be dispersing birds from population centres such as Islay. It is likely that they do not breed on Colonsay on account of the low numbers of small mammals.

Peregrine
In summer, Peregrines on Colonsay often feed on seabirds, with Kittiwakes being a favoured meal. At other times they can be found hunting almost any open ground. Sightings are usually unpredictable, but keeping a good eye on the skyline often pays dividends.

Golden Eagle
Many people have enjoyed watching Golden Eagles on Colonsay over the years – indeed the pair that were present were particularly tolerant and successfully reared young despite significant levels of disturbance. Sadly these old birds have died and have been replaced by young birds, which are more typical of the species – extremely wary and prone to disturbance. Consequently they have not been successful in producing young for over ten years; please content yourself with distant views, and if you know where they are nesting keep well away during springtime.

Sparrowhawks
Sparrowhawks can be seen almost anywhere on the islands, they are as likely to be seen hunting through the dunes on Oronsay or at Kiloran as they are to be found in Colonsay House Gardens or other woods. They are traditionally late breeders

feeding on the newly fledged young of woodland birds and up to three pairs have been known to breed in recent years around the Gardens and the spruce plantations established in the late 20th century.

Farming and Birds

There are strong links between the sympathetic farming and crofting systems used on Colonsay and Oronsay and the birds found on the islands. This applies to many species, some of which will be explored in this section; it equally applies to other groups such as the geese and also the waders, which have not been studied as closely on Colonsay as on other islands. The careful cropping patterns and attention to livestock feeding along with retention of wet areas has led to the wide range of farmland birds, some of which have disappeared from the mainland, which are still found here.

Corncrakes

The rasping call of the Corncrake is one of the harbingers of spring on Colonsay and Oronsay. They usually arrive back from their wintering grounds in Africa in late April, although individuals have been heard as early as 15 April. The precise timing of their arrival is not always easy to establish as they are such secretive birds, usually located by the distinctive call of the male (from which they get their scientific Latin name, *Crex crex*). Weather conditions have an influence on calling activity, which is restricted during periods of cold weather and when the females are incubating eggs. Thus, if conditions are poor as they arrive on the island, they can be difficult to locate. Corncrakes prefer to hide in cover and nest in long grass grown for hay and silage and it is in such areas that they are most likely to occur. This grass is a crop and is best avoided; if you want to see a Corncrake, and this is not at all easy, it is best to remain on the road or track and watch from there. The chance of seeing one is increased in spring while the vegetation is shorter.

The number of birds on the islands has varied over the years (no counts were conducted in the years with no figures):

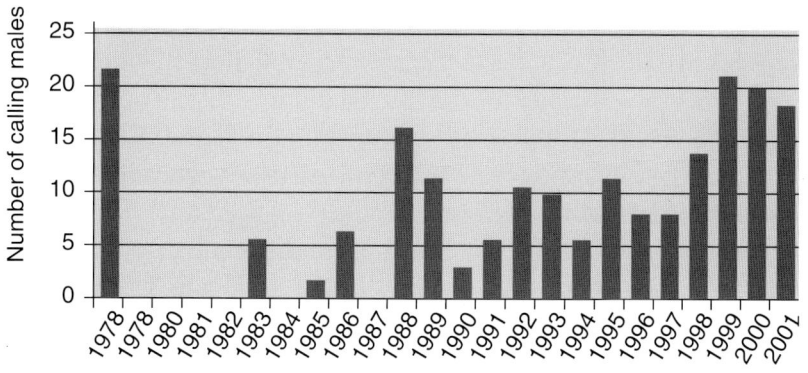

Corncrakes on Colonsay and Oronsay

The decline in Corncrakes on Colonsay and Oronsay in the 1980s was mirrored on the other Hebridean islands on which they still remained. This drop in numbers led to concern for their future and research into the factors affecting their population dynamics. While little was known about their wintering grounds and their migration, it was clear that they are relatively short lived birds that can produce large numbers of young. (Normal clutch size is 8–12 eggs). Any reduction in their breeding success could therefore have a dramatic effect on their survival. A number of factors, related to farming and crofting practice were recognized as having significant effects on breeding success.

Corncrakes, when they return in the spring need vegetation cover in which to hide and unrestricted grazing can lead to very bare pasture by late April. This is particularly true when grass growth is delayed by cold weather leading to a late spring. This problem has to some extent been overcome by fencing off "Corncrake corners" in which grazing is restricted and in other places growth of plants which provide early cover such as nettles and cow parsley has been encouraged by provision of manure. Examples of these corners can be seen in various places around the islands such as at Port Mor, Kiloran and on Oronsay.

Another problem identified was the loss of Corncrake chicks during the early harvesting of silage or hay. Young chicks, unable to fly, were killed by the cutting equipment. Two solutions were found to this problem. The first involved changes to the cutting pattern so that the inside of the field is now cut first allowing the chicks to escape, without injury, to the outside of the field. The second was to delay the cutting of the hay. This has financial implications for the crofter/farmer as the quality of the crop can decline as the autumn progresses and deteriorating weather conditions can make it harder to take in. New agri-environmental subsidies have been introduced which compensate the farmer for these losses and have helped conserve the Corncrake.

The rise in Corncrake numbers on Colonsay and Oronsay in recent years reflects the introduction of a range of positive measures on the islands. It is possible that predation of young Corncrakes by feral cats and even Hooded Crows may also affect the survival of this rare farmland bird on Colonsay, and it would be sensible to monitor any growth in population of these species. In addition to threatening the Corncrake they may seriously affect the breeding success of waders such as Lapwing.

Choughs and Other Crows
The Chough is the most beautiful, but also the rarest, crow in Britain. At present Colonsay is one of the Scottish strongholds of the species, with between 15 and 20 pairs attempting to breed. Choughs are specialist feeders eating a range of invertebrates which they dig out with their long red bills. They are social birds, often seen in flocks that roost communally. This behaviour is thought to aid their survival, as young birds can learn of good feeding areas from older birds. The Choughs on Colonsay utilise various food sources, which those on nearby Islay do not use to such a great extent. For instance, during the winter months the Chough on Colonsay can often be found at the high tide mark on beaches feeding on the grubs of the kelp flies, which feed on the rotting seaweed. In Balnahard dunes, they are often hunting out the grubs of mining bees, which live in the sandy soils of the machair.

Studies of Chough in other parts of their range in Britain and Europe have shown that they are dependent on areas of short turf for feeding. The rabbit-cropped dune systems found on Colonsay and Oronsay, with their out-wintered cattle, providing a rich source of insect food in the dung, are an ideal habitat. Chough will also hunt for food in rocky heather areas of the island and it is not uncommon to find a noisy group feeding in an area where the cattle have been present a few months previously. This close link between Chough and cattle has now been fully recognised and some farmers and conservationists are working closely to provide conditions ideal for this rare and beautiful crow.

Some of the young Chough have been fitted with colour rings as part of a larger conservation project which is monitoring their survival from year to year. This work is beginning to show that the success of the population is influenced by the survival of young birds during their first year of life, with good evidence that weather has a significant effect. This is perhaps not surprising since the Chough is only found in Britain in the warmest oceanic areas (such as Colonsay) where frosts are rare and rainfall relatively low.

There is a small population of Ravens on Colonsay, with between 7 and 10 pairs breeding every year. The tendency of some of them to attack vulnerable ewes and young lambs makes them unpopular with farmers, but this is not their only source of food. They are catholic in their taste, feeding on carrion on the shore, on cliff top beetles and also on wild bird and hen's eggs. Their re-use of traditional nesting sites every year means that monitoring of the population is relatively straightforward. Some nests regularly fail to produce young; in poor years, fewer than a third of the nests are successful, while in good years over 85% rear young. Successful nests rear on average around 2.9 young, but this can vary from year to year between 2.3 and 4.0. Some of the young do not live for long – one individual, which had been ringed in the nest, was found dead under a power-line 300m from that nest some 2 months later. A sibling of this youngster was found dead in Kintyre (66 km) the following year, providing evidence that some of the young leave the island.

Hooded Crows are now much less common than twenty years ago when a non-breeding flock of over 100 birds was regularly seen. Now there are fewer than 10 breeding pairs and a small flock of less than 20 non-breeders, as a result of a vigorous control programme.

Jackdaws are usually found in the dunes and around the cliff tops where it might be thought they would compete for food with Chough. This is not the case as Jackdaws pick their food from the surface of the ground, while Chough dig out grubs and other invertebrates with their long curved red bills.

Twite

The Twite is one of a range of small birds that live on the farmland and croft areas. It is restricted in range in Britain to upland areas and to Scotland's western and northern seaboard where it is most common. In winter it is found in small flocks in and around the farms, often close to where cattle have been feeding or on stubbles. This is where it can find the small seed on which it feeds. In summer it breeds in the heather (often on cliffs) and flies to area of short grass and weeds where it has been watched feeding on a wide range of different grasses and wildflowers such as Eyebright, Dandelion and Knapweed.

The Twite, however, is a survivor that has been able to live from the seeds of wild plants. In the late 19th and early 20th century farming on Colonsay supported a wider range of arable and root crops and other seed-eating birds, which are reliant on arable farming such as the Yellowhammer and Corn Bunting used to breed. They no longer breed because such forms of farming are only practiced in small areas, as on Oronsay where a re-introduction of these crops has seen a welcome increase in wintering finch flocks in the fields, along with some wintering Snow and Reed Buntings.

Extinct!

There is one bird which has been found on Colonsay but will never be seen again. It is the Great Auk, it was like a huge flightless Razorbill. Remains of the Great Auk were found during the archaeological excavations of the mesolithic shell middens on Oronsay by Symington Grieve in the 19th century.

Seabirds

Colonsay, lying at the mouth of the Firth of Lorne, is well situated for seabirds – it is surrounded by shallow seas, with many tidal currents that are rich in small fish. There are 14 species of seabirds which breed on Colonsay and another 5 are seen regularly. A count in 2000 showed that the total population was over 50,000 birds, meaning that Colonsay is the principal seabird centre in the Southern Inner Hebrides.

In recent years a number of studies, monitoring the populations of the various seabirds, have been undertaken. These use a series of sample sites and also the capture and re-capture of a small number of individually marked (ringed) birds. These studies have helped reveal some interesting facts about the birds which come and summer on Colonsay's cliffs.

Fulmars
Fulmars started breeding on Colonsay in 1927 and their population continued to grow through most of the century. Around 1,300 pairs were counted in the Seabird 2000 census. As it is not easy to count all the Fulmars each year a number of samples sites were counted for the 1970s and 1980s. These show that the growth of the population on Colonsay has now ceased and there is some evidence of a recent decline in the population. The reasons for this are not known; it may be because of changes in food supplies through changes in fisheries, or may be related to predation on Fulmars by Sea Eagles from Mull, or on other as yet not understood factors.

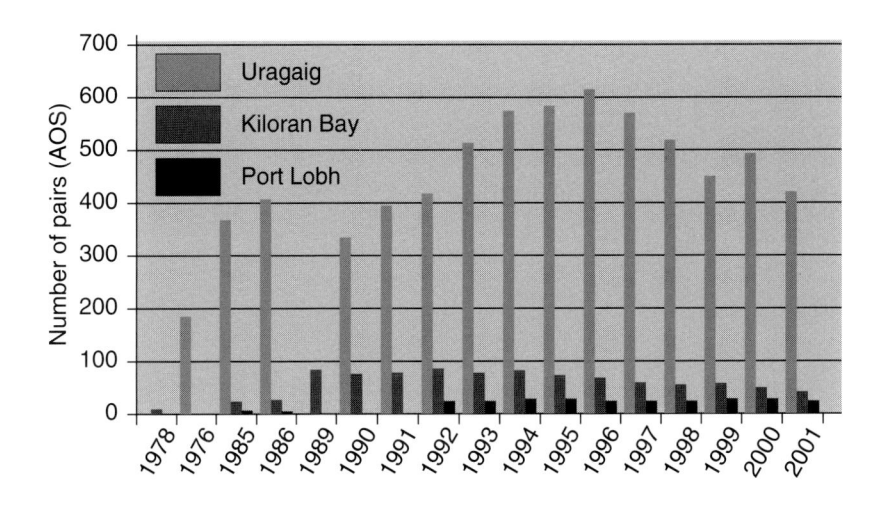

Fulmar population at sample sites on Colonsay

Guillemots

These are by far the most common seabird on Colonsay with over 26,000 being counted on the breeding ledges on the western and northern coasts of the island during June 2000. This does not include the large numbers of 'off-duty' birds sitting on the sea below the cliffs or those birds away feeding, so the population is significantly greater than this total. It was not always this size, with around half this number counted in the mid 1980s and only 1,600 in the late 1960s. A similar population increase has been noted on a number of other islands off the west coast of Scotland, such as Canna. Ringed birds from both Canna and the Treshnish Islands have been found on Colonsay showing that there is interaction between these Hebridean populations. Birds from this area spend their winters off southern Ireland, in the western approaches to the English Channel and in the Bay of Biscay. It was therefore not surprising that some of these Guillemots were found amongst the large number of dead birds washed ashore after the huge oil spill from the *Erica*, which sank in the Bay of Biscay during the Boxing Day storm of 1999.

Geriatric Guillemots

Have you ever wondered how long the seabirds at Uragaig and Pigs Paradise live? Studies using ringed birds have shown that they live much longer than might first be thought. A small sample of birds was first ringed 13 years ago in 1989 and many of these birds are still alive. Analysis of the recapture pattern of the birds allows their annual survival to be calculated. This shows that many will live to 30 years and some are likely to be older than many of the visitors to the islands.

Razorbills
Like that of Guillemots, the population of Razorbills on Colonsay almost doubled between the mid 1980s and 2000, with over 2,700 birds being counted on the cliffs in recent years. Interestingly the increase in the small number of Razorbills north of Kiloran Bay has been more marked than elsewhere. Razorbills are now more abundant than Guillemots in this piece of coastline, and tend to be found nesting in the cracks around

the edge of the cliffs. The fractured nature of the rock here is more suitable for them than the Guillemot, which prefer broader ledges. This piece of coastline also holds larger numbers of Black Guillemots whose congregations are a delight on a still early spring morning when the courtship whistles of up to 50 birds can be heard from a great distance.

Winters in the Sun!

Razorbills are not uncommon on the cliffs of Colonsay during the summer, but recent studies of ringed birds show that they are not unlike the human visitors, preferring to get a bit of winter sun. Three birds (out of 50 ringed at Pigs Paradise) have now been found in Spain during winter; a long way given there are no charter flights!

Kittiwakes
The Kittiwake is the second most common seabird on Colonsay with around 6,500 pairs being found breeding between Port Mor and Kiloran Bay in 2000. There has been little increase in the population since the mid 1980s when around 6,000 pairs were found. Just over 2,000 pairs were found in 1969, so this population has stabilised while those of Guillemot and Razorbill have continued to grow during the last 15 years. This suggests that in recent years there has been a fine balance between recruitment and survival in Kittiwakes on Colonsay; while among Guillemots and Razorbills, which tend to feed deeper underwater, recruitment is exceeding mortality and emigration.

Eskimo food

What is the connection between Kiloran Bay and Eskimos? It is the Kittiwake, the small black-legged gull, that gathers in large numbers to bathe in summer on Kiloran Bay. For these birds travel across the Atlantic to feed off Greenland in the autumn and winter. A number are killed each year for food by Eskimos, including EN95427 which was ringed at Pigs Paradise in June 1990 and recovered 2656km away in the Nuuk district of Greenland in September 1993.

The changes in the populations of some of the other gull species (Common (80 pairs), Herring (1,100pairs) and Great Black-backed Gulls (75 pairs)) on Colonsay and Oronsay have also been slight since those recorded in the mid 1980s. Black-headed Gulls are now very much rarer, with fewer than 10 pairs currently breeding, but Lesser black-backed Gulls have increased, particularly on Oronsay, to over 200 pairs.

Rarity – Black-headed Gull!

Black-headed Gulls are a common bird on the mainland, being found in close to human activity in many places. They are, however, not common on the islands with a substantial reduction in the breeding population taking place between the 1980s and the turn of the century. A small number of pairs still breed on the Strand islands and it is in this vicinity it is easiest to find them. At other times of the year than can be equally scarce and it is possible to go for days without seeing them during mid-winter.

Checklist & Status

This checklist gives details of the whole range of species that have confirmed records for Colonsay and Oronsay since 1975. In total 191 species have been noted during this period and species are being added annually as more birdwatchers visit the islands.

Please pass on details of your records which show a change in the status of any species to the Argyll County Bird recorder or email them to the author @ dcjardine@freeuk.co.uk.

Key to Abundance and Status

Abundance	*No of birds per year*	*Abbreviation*
Abundant	> 10,000	**A**
Common	1001 – 10,000	**C**
Well Represented	101 – 1000	**WR**
Uncommon	11 – 100	**U**
Rare	1–10	**R**
Extremely Rare	< 1	**E**

Status	*Abbreviation*
Breeder	**B**
Previously bred	**HB**
Passage Migrant	**P**
Winter Visitor	**WV**
Vagrant	**V**

Species	Abundance	Status
Red-throated Diver	U	B
Black-throated Diver	R	P
Great Northern Diver	U	WV
Little Grebe	U	B
Red-necked Grebe	ER	V
Slavonian Grebe	R	WV
Fulmar	C	B
Great Shearwater	ER	V
Sooty Shearwater	U	P
Manx Shearwater	WR	P
Storm Petrel	U	PM
Leach's Petrel	ER	V
Gannet	C	P
Cormorant	U	WV
Shag	WR	B
Grey Heron	U	B
Mute Swan	ER	P
Whooper Swan	U	WV
Pink-footed Goose	R	WV
White-fronted Goose	WR	WV
Greylag Goose	WR	B
Snow Goose	ER	P
Canada Goose	U	B
Barnacle Goose	WR	WV
Brent Goose	R	P
Shelduck	U	B
Wigeon	U	WV
Gadwall	ER	WV
Teal	WR	B
Mallard	WR	B
Pintail	R	WV
Garganey	ER	V
Shoveler	R	HB
Pochard	U	WV
Tufted Duck	U	B
Scaup	R	WV

Species	Abundance	Status
Eider	WR	B
Long-tailed Duck	R	WV
Common Scoter	R	WV
Goldeneye	U	WV
Smew	ER	V
Red-breasted Merganser	U	B
Goosander	R	WV
Honey Buzzard	ER	V
White-tailed Eagle	R	WV
Hen Harrier	U	WV
Sparrowhawk	U	B
Buzzard	WR	B
Golden Eagle	R	B
Osprey	ER	P
Kestrel	R	HB
Merlin	U	HB
Peregrine	U	B
Red Grouse	R	HB
Red-legged Partridge	R	HB
Quail	ER	V
Pheasant	WR	B
Water Rail	R	B
Spotted Crake	ER	V
Corncrake	U	B
Moorhen	R	HB
Coot	R	HB
Oystercatcher	WR	B
Ringed Plover	WR	B
Killdeer	ER	V
Dotterel	ER	V
American Golden Plover	ER	V
Golden Plover	WR	WV
Grey Plover	R	P
Lapwing	WR	B
Knot	R	P
Sanderling	U	WV

Species	Abundance	Status
Little Stint	ER	P
Curlew Sandpiper	ER	P
Purple Sandpiper	R	WV
Dunlin	WR	B
Ruff	ER	P
Jack Snipe	R	WV
Snipe	WR	B
Woodcock	U	B
Black-tailed Godwit	U	P
Bar-tailed Godwit	U	WV
Whimbrel	U	P
Curlew	WR	WV
Redshank	WR	B
Greenshank	U	WV
Green Sandpiper	R	P
Wood Sandpiper	ER	P
Common Sandpiper	WR	B
Turnstone	U	WV
Grey Phalarope	ER	P
Pomarine Skua	ER	P
Arctic Skua	U	P
Great Skua	R	P
Little Gull	ER	V
Sabine's Gull	ER	V
Black-headed Gull	U	B
Common Gull	WR	B
Lesser Black-backed Gull	WR	B
Herring Gull	C	B
Iceland Gull	R	WV
Glaucous Gull	ER	WV
Great Black-backed Gull	WR	B
Kittiwake	A	B
Sandwich Tern	R	P
Common Tern	U	B
Arctic Tern	WR	B
Little Tern	R	B

Species	Abundance	Status
Black Tern	ER	V
Guillemot	A	B
Razorbill	C	B
Black Guillemot	WR	B
Little Auk	R	WV
Puffin	R	P
Rock Dove	WR	B
Stock Dove	ER	V
Woodpigeon	U	B
Collared Dove	U	B
Turtle Dove	ER	B
Cuckoo	U	B
Barn Owl	ER	WV
Tawny Owl	ER	V
Long-eared Owl	R	B
Short-eared Owl	ER	V
Swift	R	P
Great Spotted Woodpecker	ER	HB
Skylark	C	B
Sand Martin	R	P
Swallow	U	B
House Martin	R	HB
Tree Pipit	ER	P
Meadow Pipit	A	B
Rock Pipit	WR	B
Blue-headed Wagtail	ER	P
Grey Wagtail	R	WV
Pied Wagtail	WR	B
Waxwing	ER	WV
Dipper	R	P
Wren	C	B
Dunnock	WR	B
Robin	C	B
Redstart	ER	P
Whinchat	U	B
Stonechat	WR	B

Species	Abundance	Status
Wheatear	WR	B
Ring Ouzel	ER	P
Blackbird	WR	B
Fieldfare	WR	WV
Song Thrush	C	B
Redwing	WR	WV
Mistle Thrush	U	B
Grasshopper Warbler	R	B
Sedge Warbler	U	B
Reed Warbler	ER	V
Lesser Whitethroat	ER	V
Whitethroat	U	B
Garden Warbler	R	HB
Blackcap	R	B
Wood Warbler	R	HB
Chiffchaff	U	B
Willow Warbler	C	B
Goldcrest	WR	B
Spotted Flycatcher	U	B
Pied Flycatcher	ER	P
Long-tailed Tit	U	HB
Coal Tit	WR	B
Blue Tit	WR	B
Great Tit	U	B
Treecreeper	U	B
Chough	U	B
Jackdaw	WR	B
Rook	R	WV
Hooded Crow	U	B
Raven	U	B
Starling	C	B
House Sparrow	WR	B
Chaffinch	WR	B
Brambling	ER	WV
Greenfinch	U	B
Goldfinch	R	HB

Species	Abundance	Status
Siskin	U	P
Linnet	WR	B
Twite	WR	B
Redpoll	U	B
Common Crossbill	R	P
Bullfinch	R	HB
Scarlet Rosefinch	ER	V
Lapland Bunting	ER	V
Snow Bunting	R	WV
Yellowhammer	R	HB
Reed Bunting	U	B
Red-headed Bunting	ER	V
Corn Bunting	ER	V

Stop Press: in August 2002 the British Birds Rarities Committee confirmed the following:

| Black-headed Bunting | ER | V |

Argyll Bird Club

The Argyll Bird Club plays an active part in the promotion of ornithology in Argyll. It holds two one-day meetings each year at different venues in the county and organises field trips for members. It also publishes the annual *Argyll Bird Report* and a quarterly members' newsletter, *The Eider*, which includes details of club activities and articles by members and others.

Your sightings of birds on Colonsay and Oronsay are important. Individual sightings and counts of birds are helpful in their conservation as they help identify trends in their status. Please send details of your sightings to the Club local recorder: Paul Daw, Tigh-na-Tulloch, Tullochgorm, Minard, Inveraray, PA32 8YQ.

Further reading

While it is hoped that this booklet will help you understand more about Colonsay's Birds, there are a number of other sources available for those who wish to delve more deeply. The following publications are recommended:

Argyll Bird Reports 1–16 (1984–2000) Argyll Bird Club.
Gathorne Hardy A E (1914) *My Happy Hunting Grounds.* Longmans, Green & Co. London.
Jardine D C, Clarke J & Clarke PM (1985) *The Birds of Colonsay and Oransay.*
Jardine D C, How J, Clarke J &Clarke PM (*in press*) Seabirds on Colonsay and Oronsay, Inner Hebrides. Scottish Birds
Loder J De V (1935) *Colonsay and Oronsay in the Isles of Argyll: Their history, flora, fauna and topography.* Oliver & Boyd, Edinburgh and London.
McNeill M (1910) *Colonsay – one of the Hebrides.* D Douglas, Edinburgh. *Reprinted House of Lochar (2001).*
Murray F (1887) *Summer in the Hebrides.* Maclehose & Sons, Glasgow. *Reprinted by Colonsay Books (1994).*
Waltho C M (2001) 'Eider in the Firth of Clyde: a 20th century success story'. In *Conference on the ecology and management of the Firth of Clyde* held at U.B.M.S. Millport under the auspices of the Firth of Clyde Forum, Scottish Natural Heritage, Edinburgh, pp19–23.